The CHRISTMAS STORY

About the Illustrator:

Cathy Ann Johnson received her BFA from Columbus College of Art and Design, in Columbus, OH. She has one child, a son, named Clinton Love, and their home is in Kansas City, Missouri. *The Christmas Story* is Cathy Ann Johnson's nineteenth children's book.

Copyright © 1999 by Tommy Nelson

Published in Nashville, Tennessee, by Tommy Nelson™, a division of Thomas Nelson, Inc.

Scripture quoted from the *International Children's Bible, New Century Version,* © 1986, 1988, 1999 by Tommy Nelson™, a division of Thomas Nelson, Inc. Used by permission.

Library of Congress Cataloging-in-Publication Data
Bible. English. New Century. Selections. 1999.
    The story of Christmas : from the Gospels of Matthew and Luke / illustrated
by Cathy Ann Johnson.
        p. cm.
    "Scripture quoted from the International Children's Bible, New Century
Version"—T.p. verso
    Summary: A simple retelling of the Nativity story.
    ISBN 0-8499-7528-X
    [1. Jesus Christ—Nativity. 2. Bible stories—N.T.] I. Johnson, Cathy (Cathy
A.) ill. II. Title.
BT315.A3 1999
232.92—dc21
                                                            99-23700
                                                            CIP

Printed in the United States of America
99 00 01 02 03 QPH 9 8 7 6 5 4 3 2 1

The CHRISTMAS STORY

From the Gospels
of Matthew and Luke

Illustrated by
CATHY ANN JOHNSON

Tommy NELSON

Thomas Nelson, Inc.
Nashville

God sent the angel Gabriel to a virgin who lived in Nazareth, a town in Galilee. She was engaged to marry a man named Joseph from the family of David. Her name was Mary. The angel came to her and said, "Greetings! The Lord has blessed you and is with you."

But Mary was very confused by what the angel said. Mary wondered, "What does this mean?"

Luke 1:26–29

The angel said to her, "Don't be afraid, Mary, because God is pleased with you. Listen! You will become pregnant. You will give birth to a son, and you will name him Jesus. He will be great, and people will call him the Son of the Most High. The Lord God will give him the throne of King David, his ancestor. He will rule over the people of Jacob forever. His kingdom will never end."

Mary said to the angel, "How will this happen? I am a virgin!"

The angel said to Mary, "The Holy Spirit will come upon you, and the power of the Most High will cover you. The baby will be holy. He will be called the Son of God.

Mary said, "I am the servant girl of the Lord. Let this happen to me as you say!" Then the angel went away.

Luke 1:30–35, 38

And this is how the birth of Jesus came about.
Mary . . . learned that she was going to have a baby.
She was pregnant by the power of the Holy Spirit. . . .
Joseph was a good man. He did not want to disgrace
her in public, so he planned to divorce her secretly.

Matthew 1:18–19

While Joseph thought about this, an angel of the Lord came to him in a dream. The angel said, "Joseph, descendant of David, don't be afraid to take Mary as your wife. The baby in her is from the Holy Spirit. She will give birth to a son. You will name the son Jesus. Give him that name because he will save his people from their sins."

When Joseph woke up, he did what the Lord's angel had told him to do. Joseph married Mary.

Matthew 1:20–21, 24

At that time, Augustus Caesar sent an order to all people in the countries that were under Roman rule. The order said that they must list their names in a register. This was the first registration taken while Quirinius was governor of Syria. And everyone went to their own towns to be registered.

So Joseph left Nazareth, a town in Galilee. He went to the town of Bethlehem in Judea. This town was known as the town of David. Joseph went there because he was from the family of David. Joseph registered with Mary. . . .

Luke 2:1–5

While Joseph and Mary were in Bethlehem, the time came for her to have the baby. She gave birth to her first son. There were no rooms left in the inn. So she wrapped the baby with cloths and laid him in a box where animals are fed.

Luke 2:6–7

That night, some shepherds were in the fields nearby watching their sheep. An angel of the Lord stood before them. The glory of the Lord was shining around them, and suddenly they became very frightened. The angel said to them, "Don't be afraid, because I am bringing you some good news. It will be a joy to all the people. Today your Savior was born in David's town. He is Christ, the Lord. This is how you will know him: You will find a baby wrapped in cloths and lying in a feeding box."

Luke 2:8–12

Then a very large group of angels from heaven joined the first angel. All the angels were praising God, saying:

"Give glory to God in heaven,
and on earth let there be peace
to the people who please God."

Then the angels left the shepherds and went back to heaven.

Luke 2:13–15

The shepherds said to each other, "Let us go to Bethlehem and see this thing that has happened. We will see this thing the Lord told us about."

So the shepherds went quickly and found Mary and Joseph. And the shepherds saw the baby lying in a feeding box. Then they told what the angels had said about this child. Everyone was amazed when they heard what the shepherds said to them.

Mary hid these things in her heart; she continued to think about them. Then the shepherds went back to their sheep, praising God and thanking him for everything that they had seen and heard. It was just as the angel had told them.

Luke 2:15–20

Jesus was born . . . during the time when Herod was king. After Jesus was born, some wise men from the east came to Jerusalem. They asked, "Where is the baby who was born to be the king of the Jews? We saw his star in the east. We came to worship him."

When King Herod heard about this new king of the Jews, he was troubled. And all the people in Jerusalem were worried too. Herod called a meeting of all the leading priests and teachers of the law. He asked them where the Christ would be born. They answered, "In the town of Bethlehem in Judea. . . ."

Then Herod had a secret meeting with the wise men from the east. He learned from them the exact time they first saw the star. Then Herod sent the wise men to Bethlehem. He said to them, "Go and look carefully to find the child. When you find him, come tell me. Then I can go worship him too."

Matthew 2:1–5, 7–8

The wise men heard the king and then left. They saw the same star they had seen in the east. It went before them until it stopped above the place where the child was.

Matthew 2:9

When the wise men saw the star, they were filled with joy. They went to the house where the child was and saw him with his mother, Mary. They bowed down and worshiped the child. They opened the gifts they brought for him. They gave him treasures of gold, frankincense, and myrrh. But God warned the wise men in a dream not to go back to Herod. So they went home to their own country by a different way.

Matthew 2:10–12

"For God loved the world so much that he gave his only Son. God gave his Son so that whoever believes in him may not be lost, but have eternal life. . . ."

John 3:16